A book of
poetic prose

TOTEM
DARREN NEILSEN

Totem © 2025 Darren Neilsen

All Rights Reserved. No part of this book may be reproduced in any form or by any electronic or mechanical means including information storage and retrieval systems, without permission in writing from the author. The only exception is by a reviewer, who may quote short excerpts in a review.

No generative artifical intelligence (AI) was used in the creation of this book. The author expressly prohibits the use of this publication as training data for AI technologies or large language models (LLMs) for generative purposes. The author reserves all rights to license uses of this work for generative AI training and the development of LLMs.

This book is a work of fiction. Names, characters, places, and incidents either are products of the author's imagination or are used fictitiously. Any resemblance to actual persons, living or dead, events, or locales is entirely coincidental.

Printed in Australia

Cover and internal design by Coven Press

www.covenpress.com.au

First printing: August 2025

Paperback ISBN 978-0-6451214-4-5

eBook ISBN 978-0-6451214-6-9

 A catalogue record for this work is available from the National Library of Australia

Distributed by Lightning Source Global

ALSO BY THE AUTHOR

On Dark Wings – Collected Poetry

For Kristy
You light up my world

FOREWORD

This second collection of poetry was written between 2006 and 2025. When I think of those twenty years, I see a lot of my life (mostly good) with my wonderful wife Kristy, I've had three amazing children, run a business (again, mostly good), resurrected my amateur baseball career, become an amateur photographer, all while trying to finish a novel but constantly returning to short stories and poetry time and again. Many of these poems began life as scrawled passages on white paper pie bags at work, others as notes in my phone.

If my first book, *On Dark Wings*, was my younger self, searching for my voice, then these poems sum me up more as the poet I have become. I can see the change in style over the years, with the form and the flow becoming smoother and a little more mature. I can see my confidence with the words, and how I fit them together. There are arcs that continue from the first collection, in the Sally poems, the Memory poems, and the Phoenix poems. There is also a couple of subtle Westreach poems tucked in for good measure.

I feel that these poems are a little stronger, a little more balanced, but just as deep and immersive as those in the first collection. They were written with an entire array of emotions, but often as a way to clear the noise in my head. I am proud of these poems and so very glad that they will finally be published with the technical help from Coven Press.

I would like to credit such renowned Poets as Judith

Wright, Judith Beveridge, Bruce Dawe, Ted Hughes, T.S Elliot, and so many others, for the impact they had on a young writer honing his craft.

The last poem in this collection, fittingly, was written by my steadfast and stoic Father. He is the earliest evidence I can find of my need/desire to write. I credit his Sunday morning stories, and also his love of country music (John Williamson, Slim Dusty, Kenny Rogers among others) and how much of a story the lyrics often told. The first thing I ever wrote was a horrible little country song. I'm comfortable in saying my writing has improved since then. I hope you enjoy this collection of poetry as much as I did writing them.

As always, stay kind,
Darren Neilsen

CONTENTS

vii	Foreword
1	Dragonflies and Spiders
2	Earth Song
3	Real Words
4	The Phoenix Revenge
5	Anna Dreams the Seasons
6	Turtle – A Memory Poem
8	Visiting Loved Ones with Sunflowers
9	In Thought of Crows
11	Alyssa
12	Like Tree Bark
13	Night Driving
14	The Spirit Tree
15	The August Song
16	Huntress – A Memory Poem
18	Certain Seasons
19	Old Betty
21	Modern Barriers
22	Fire Tree
23	Something Has Died
24	Outback Dreaming
25	On Grief
26	Dark Aura – A Memory Poem
27	Voices in the Wind
28	Mr Eternal
29	Sunsets and Dragonflies

30	A September Sunday
31	Totemless
32	Belinda
33	The Divided – A Memory Poem
35	Eternal Crow
36	Scorched Clean
37	Echoes of Atlantis
38	The Dust of Ages
39	With Clarity
40	Something I Know for Sure
41	Andrew's Son
42	Avian Dance – A Memory Poem
43	The Distant Echo of Thunder
44	Sam's Song
45	Sacrifice
47	Sally's Prayer
48	An Eternal Queen
50	Late on a Sunday
51	On Calvary Hill
52	Wounds of the Mind
54	Leviathan – A Memory Poem
55	Revenants of Youth
57	Immortal – A Memory Poem
59	The Last Day of History
60	Blackened Leaves
61	Leaving Hospital Hopes
64	Dream Gates
65	Kyproulla's Garden
67	City Silent
68	Sunset Silhouettes
69	An October Dirge
70	Memory – A Memory Poem

71	Secrets
72	The Dark Between the Stars
74	Pedestal
75	Silent Angel
77	An Understated Anthem
78	Green Crow
79	Those Who Were Left Behind
80	Every Breath is a Circle
81	Sally
82	Crow – A Memory Poem
83	Childhood Vignette
85	The Phoenix Redemption
86	In Triumph
87	Endings and Beginnings – A Memory Poem
89	Don't Live Your Life Like a Dirge
91	Runways
93	Urban Mythology
94	The Black Cathedral
96	Windrush

DRAGONFLIES AND SPIDERS

Life is an ember
burning high on a southern wind.

Elise finds herself,
standing on a beach at dusk,
thinking about the friends
that she has lost.
The sand is warm around her feet
and her memories betray her,
freeing tears to trace their way
slowly down her face.
She finds herself wondering
if she had done things differently,
how her life would be.
She gets caught in the confusion
of regret and self-doubt,
still trying to find the answers,
to questions she need not ask.

It saddens her,
because she doesn't get to the beach much,
yet when she does, she thinks of Nathan,
and she smiles a little.

Death comes to all things,
dragonflies and spiders are no exception.

EARTH SONG

Herman Melville tells me
that everything has a voice,
and that nature's voice is musical.
I try to imagine the sound of that song
and get lost in the thought
of churches and homeless people
and everything else I think about
when I come into the city.

Herman Melville tells us
that everything has a voice.
Maybe we should listen.

REAL WORDS

Sally tries to remember
what it felt like to be loved.
She tries to recall
what it meant to have a home.
She cannot comprehend
the warmth behind words
such as family,
love,
and solace.

Sally dwells in the real world
with real words
like cold,
desperate,
and hope.

Sally keeps a small blue dictionary in her pocket.
One day she hopes to understand.

THE PHOENIX REVENGE

In the aftermath of his own downfall,
he made man from the last piece of ash
and the gleam in his obsidian eye.
He gave to it all his pride, pain, and anguish,
then threw it back into the embers and flew away,
cursing every tree and mountain, river and ocean,
leaving behind him only whispers upon the wind
that spoke of a creator.

ANNA DREAMS THE SEASONS

Anna sees Autumn as having long brown hair
flecked with orange and yellow and red.
She describes a narrow, pointed face
with kind dark eyes that do not judge.

Anna thinks of Winter as a handsome man in his twenties,
jet black hair and cool blue eyes.
She paints a solitary expression upon his face
and believes that he would rarely speak.

Anna draws Spring to look like a bimbo,
blue-eyed and blonde haired, big-boobed and baby faced.
She finds a hidden intelligence within those eyes,
so vibrantly deep and full of life.

Anna believes that Summer has a hard face
beneath red hair that shimmers as he moves.
She stares at the empty canvas for hours
trying to capture that image of heat.

TURTLE – A MEMORY POEM

Distance trails behind him
like a dream he need not remember.
Time trails behind like distance,
yet complicated and purposeful,
like his twisted insides.
His eyes are wide and glassy,
and his view of the world
is superimposed by another
stained with darkness
and burning with incandescent lights
that flicker and dance around him.
For decades,
he has been translating them,
searching for the answers.
He has doubts in his ability to do so,
and this causes fear to swell within,
because he can see
that the shadow of darkness is rising.

He sits on a low brick wall
with his feet swinging unconsciously.
Beside him is a bag full of textbooks,
forgotten or ignored,
for his thoughts are elsewhere.
His eyes are wide and glassy

and he is beginning to understand,
that once again,
the shadow of darkness is rising.

VISITING LOVED ONES WITH SUNFLOWERS

Late December,
though it feels like autumn
beneath a cool breeze that sifts
through the leaves
of wide branched trees.
In a summer dress,
with a handful of flowers
she walks narrow grassed corridors,
looking for loved ones.

She pauses, beset by memories
that will fade but never leave.
A teardrop sky surrounds her,
and she brushes dirt and leaves
from the spaces between letters
that spell her grandmother's name.

IN THOUGHT OF CROWS

There's a kid in a park somewhere,
looking up at the city skyline
high above the trees.

He's got a crumpled packet of cigarettes,
issues at home and a junkie girlfriend,
but he takes it all with him when he leaves.

Suicidal mother, violent father,
and a younger brother who can't stop stealing,
make it hard for him to believe.

Yet he knows there's something better,
he sees it in the depth of that open sky,
so clear and blue and unable to deceive.

Of all the turmoil, the pain, and the crap
that has turned his life this way,
his innocence is the one thing he still grieves.

But staring at the sky as a crow lifts into flight
there is nothing if there is not hope.
That is the one thing he can concede.

To imagine himself in an avian state
with wings black and shimmering blue,
flying over cities, over mountains, over rivers, over seas.

On the soul's ecstatic journey
upon winds of pure light,
he rises, he changes and then he flees.

ALYSSA

From a window to the spirit world,
in the corner of the maternity room,
three grandmothers watch as our daughter
makes her way into the world.

On the way home from the hospital,
a white butterfly follows us and flutters around our car.
Some welcoming angel, or protective totem
come to make Alyssa's acquaintance.

Later, we stand together and watch her sleep.
And when she wakes from vivid dreams
of big cats, butterflies, and beautiful lives,
I hope she knows that we will always be with her.

LIKE TREE BARK

Sally tells me
that the sky seems too blue,
the sunlight overly bright,
and the birdsong extra chirpy today.

She tells me
that the leaves on the trees are so green
that it hurts her eyes to look at them.

Sally tells me all this
with a shy smile on her face.
It makes me believe
that all the hard times she's been through
have not broken her,
but somehow made her stronger.

NIGHT DRIVING

Driving around,
we listen to Oasis
and talk about homeless people,
old girlfriends,
and all the things we'll do when we're older.

Night driving
is like existing
in a different universe.
You used to tell me this all the time,
and I never really understood,
that there was a world
outside of work and coffee
and sadness and depression
and all that other shit.

Driving home,
I listen to the radio
and talk to myself
about all the things
that I would change if I could.

THE SPIRIT TREE

Those wide welcoming branches
await me when I close my eyes.
Heavy leaves move like subtle dancers
beneath the cold fingers of winter,
and etched in the smooth bark of its trunk
are all the secrets of the world.
Beneath an eternal sunrise,
this endless spread of pink and orange sky,
stags and serpents are seen between the exposed roots.

I walk peacefully,
circling the world tree.
Beneath the blowing spirit wind
I hear a whisper which sings of hope,
and tells me
that every day is valuable,
every word is powerful,
and every dream can be fulfilled.

THE AUGUST SONG

Deep in slumber,
your features soft and carefree as a picture
that is the song of all my pride and love.

Standing over you,
it seems a shame to wake you
but for the promise I made last night.

Cold morning,
the sky becoming azure
and your eyes wide at the sight of it.

From the clifftop we look out over the water,
and the clouds take to colour
as the sun begins to rise.

The constant waves are soothing,
the air is fresh from the sea,
and everything is in this moment.

In the August song
everything is as it should be
and everyone belongs.

HUNTRESS – A MEMORY POEM

Growing restless,
the lioness paces towards the mountain,
where even the gods go to worship.
She recognises that something ominous
has drawn her to this majestic place,
yet she cannot comprehend that power.
She knows it only by the foulness
that invades her senses.
At the mountain's base
she lays, prostrate,
and remains throughout the day,
giving all the respect due
to the ancient stone giant.
At dusk,
she starts upon its lower slopes
where the jungle remains.
She makes her way beneath the canopy,
cautiously scanning the undergrowth.
She traces an old path to higher ground
and makes her way onto the stony slope.
She pauses and offers another prayer
as she comes across the bones of an elephant,
tusks pointing savagely
higher up the mountain.

*

She peers through the camera,
sees the world through another eye.
In that instant she finds herself torn between two places.
She sees the world through cat's eyes,
this stretched landscape, dark and grey.
There is a beauty to it that she cannot explain.
She wishes she could capture it in print,
this emotion that makes her cry at night
knowing that with every morning,
she wakes a little less than she was the day before.
Strangely, between tears,
she finds herself attempting to pray.

CERTAIN SEASONS

Late at night
she sits alone in the backyard,
quietly smoking cigarettes.
She thinks about the past,
wondering, if occasionally,
it could have gone a different way.

And occasionally, in certain seasons,
I look up at the stars
in a dark, clear sky
and wonder how things would be
if they had gone a different way.

It's been so long since I've seen her,
and I watch as that smile I remember
begins to grow again.
I see a woman,
where I only knew the girl.
And it makes me proud,
to see that same light in her eyes.

OLD BETTY

You see old Betty around Sydney,
pushing a shopping trolley
that holds all of her worldly possessions.
Her face has gone to wrinkles
and her eyes have started to go.
If you ever stop to talk to her,
she'll tell you that she worships the gods
of concrete, metal, and glass.
She prays to them for handouts, free food,
and something to smile about.
Even if you ignore her words,
you can still hear her as she talks to herself
about the current economic situation
and the lack of social compassion
that has put her where she is.
And how, most of all
she wishes she had someone else to talk to.

On cold nights she mumbles,
trying to recall what her life was like before,
when she had everything she thought she needed.
I know this, because on those cold nights,
when we all gather with our blankets and sleeping bags
on the steps across from Town Hall,
and as I try to convince myself that it's okay to sleep,

I listen to her words and try to find the answers
that will explain all the inconsistencies of human nature.

MODERN BARRIERS

Claire tells me to live
and to be honest with myself
as much as I can.
She speaks in lyrics.
It's a barrier that she has created
to protect herself
against everything that could compete
with the solidarity of her mind.

I tell her to live
and to be honest with herself,
because I cannot.

FIRE TREE

Fire Tree burns like a heart,
ablaze with love or self destruction.
Ribbons of flame lap the bark and engulf the leaves,
raising sweet smelling smoke
that goes against the vivid image of awesome nature.
You are as one with the tree,
but watching from a distance.
The flames feed off your fears and insecurities,
leaving you hollow and waiting
for something new to fill you,
or something lost to return.
Stand tall,
for all that is broken is not gone,
and all that is done is behind you.

SOMETHING HAS DIED

The last day begins with a perfect blue sky.

An eerie and almighty chorus of crows
drowns out all other sound.
People walk barefoot from their homes,
stand on hot concrete,
shade their eyes and look to a darkening sky.
Feathers drift in the furore,
fall like autumn leaves
then crumple on the ground like ash.
Without words,
the onlookers are suddenly aware
that somewhere,
something has died.

OUTBACK DREAMING

With hanging strips of bark
like carefully peeled skin,
the oldest tree resembles an aged man.

A thinness, a bushland dry,
upon a sigh of wind through twisting leaves,
leaves you silent,
caught in a poignant moment,
stumbling through the memories of a childhood
raised on red-dust and open plains,
bush wattles and billabongs.

See the dust storm gathering strength,
stout houses bent beneath harsh nature,
that a painter describes with hot red ochre
and smears of charcoal.

In a dried-up outback town
there's an old man,
tanned and weathered features,
like the worn bark of a tree
you played near in your youth.

ON GRIEF

Grief is a ribbon that runs around our fingers,
up our arms and through our torso.
It tightens and tightens,
spreading like tentacles through our guts and minds,
stitching old wounds into new flesh.
It will consume us if we let it,
strangle us from the inside out like silence.
Grief was meant as a process to say farewell.
It is here to be felt and then released.
It was never meant to be a standard of living.

DARK AURA - A MEMORY POEM

Cautious and watchful,
she passes through society unnoticed,
just below the surface.
As she constantly surveys her surroundings,
something sharp can be seen shining
in those cold, calculating eyes.
There is an aura of malignancy about her
that keeps people at a distance.
Within the corporate world,
it is eat or be eaten,
and she made a vow long ago,
never to show mercy.

Under the water
the world is an entirely different place.
The lords of survival dwell beneath the surface,
patient, omnipresent, and forever watchful.
In those murky waters it is known
that man is not the only hunter
who preys upon his own.
The realm of the crocodile is harsh,
consumed by violence,
and knows no mercy.

VOICES IN THE WIND

The clouds hang low in an overcast sky,
dark and ominously malignant.
Wind blows litter and dust in a dance
around deserted playground equipment.
Sally sits with a purple shoebox,
taped shut with duct tape.
She plays with a piece that has twisted and lost its stick.
Her thoughts are in the past
and her eyes try to penetrate
all the pain and desolation before her
to see back to those days
where happiness was not a stranger.

Sally thinks about opening the shoebox,
but can do so only as much
as she can take herself back to those carefree times.
She moves slowly on a swing,
listening for voices in the wind.

MR ETERNAL

wakes in a panic most days
unsure of where he is
and what shape the world is,
but the feeling slowly settles
like silt in a bottle of water
and eventually he starts to smile,
for he knows that each day is a gift,
each smile is priceless,
and even rainy days are something to be thankful for.

SUNSETS AND DRAGONFLIES

Jocelyn talks of archways and cornices
with a passion that blazes in her eyes.
It is a fever of the soul that completes her,
if anyone will listen or look.
She likes sunsets and dragonflies,
dances in the rain when she remembers to.
Takes slow walks around the city on Sundays
and revels in the architecture and the artistry.
On quiet nights, she reminisces of conversations
held with her father after dinners
when they would talk about buildings
and concrete things like love, confidence, faith and hope.

A SEPTEMBER SUNDAY

She farewelled another friend,
and the weight of such goodbyes
resides within her like an anchor.
Don't go, she whispers slowly,
to the early spring sunset.
Yet still she feels the cold of August
in her hands and in her heart.
The blue sky taunts her with beauty,
birdsong echoes the eternal call of heaven,
and somewhere inside,
something strong is telling her
Be strong, for life continues.

TOTEMLESS

I wait,
for skies to shrink within themselves.
Alone, hungry, weary, and fearful,
I pray for new beginnings,
or endings to be undone.

Here on the edge of everything,
and nothing,
I wait like a broken clock,
like a purple bruise,
like the last pent breath,
thriving on the knowledge that someday
something will become.

Totemless, I wait,
for skies to expand beyond themselves
extending into everything that was or will be.

Maybe as the sun rises...

BELINDA

I remember,
shining beauty, bright eyes,
and a loving smile.
It was visible to every eye,
that she was special.
We all saw her warmth of spirit,
that light that burned within.

Your grief is,
and will remain,
a remnant of how much you loved her.

Memories are eternal,
and the heart is a palace
of strength and hope.
Her happiness will stay with you
even after the memories fade.

THE DIVIDED – A MEMORY POEM

He wakes in a strange house
next to an unfamiliar woman,
and for the alcohol he had consumed,
cannot remember the night before.
Looking upon her,
he knows that there is something he should remember.
The sunlight through the window
casts stripes across her naked back,
dapples the floor with shadows
that blur before his sight.
It makes him think of the jungle
that echoes in his dreams.

Slow, cautious, calculated.
A spirit made of flesh,
stalking through the undergrowth.
The tiger stops suddenly,
meticulously scans the trees and dense foliage
for the source of the scent that has invaded the jungle.
The taste of evil reaches the tiger's nose
and sets old fears aflame.
Distantly,
the tiger finds himself peering into a twisted future
where he is broken in two.

*

She sees him in the nightclub
and recognises in him,
that lost piece of herself.
There is a bond between them
as though they are born of the same soul.
But in this cold impartial world,
she does not understand the connection,
and only acts upon it.
She takes him home
and while they're having sex
she finds herself thinking of the jungle once more.

ETERNAL CROW

Against the face of a golden orb
that is settling over stone sentinels,
a dark silhouette traces a path.

A black winged bird flies into the west,
rendering the world into shades of pink and red and grey.
He brings the night behind him like an old cloak,
with crystalline stars that are simply holes in the cloth
that we can see through to a better place.
The beat of his wings mimics the beat of our hearts
as we kneel to pray in the evening,
asking for forgiveness, happiness, and hope.
Unlike the rest of us,
he cannot stop.

Towards a flaming orange ball
that is melting into majestic mountains,
a black winged bird flies forever.

SCORCHED CLEAN

Sally tells me
that she wants to see it all
burnt to the ground.
There is something about the idea,
she says,
of those yellow and orange flames
consuming all of the hate
and pain and fear
that has overtaken the city.
She tells me of another world,
scorched clean by monumental fire,
where greed and loneliness
no longer exist.

I'm scared for her,
but the passion and hope in her eyes
leads me to believe,
that maybe,
just maybe,
she might be on the right track.

ECHOES OF ATLANTIS

Izzy speaks of Atlantis,
without even knowing that she does.
I know this, I can see the light in her eyes.

At eight,
the world seems so huge
and I can understand
how eager she is
to find out how it all works.

I try to tell her
that the answers she searches for
are not the answers she will find.
I keep trying to find ways
to tell her to stay young,
without making her feel like a child.

So many wonderful things await,
and I cannot wait to watch her try them,
but for now, I'll tell her to enjoy what she has
and look forward to what is to come.

The light in Izzy's eyes shines through
like echoes of Atlantis.

THE DUST OF AGES

There is graffiti on the walls of Valhalla,
and in the castle courtyard there are crows
perched in the twisted branches of a dead tree
like squatters who would not be made to leave.

The dust of ages covers everything.
Undecided winds lift it into the air
to dance in small spirals
that mean nothing and go nowhere.

The memories of mythology fade,
yet in the afterglow of mystery
there is a sense of recognition
that we are all part of a larger picture.

When the paint flakes and falls away from the battlements,
and the dust of ages departs,
the crows will call out in awe
as Yggdrasil blooms again.

WITH CLARITY

The sky is awash with pale rippled clouds,
the sunset turns them golden.
The streets are quiet,
and the static in your mind is subsiding
and you're starting to think
that maybe you'll sleep tonight.
All these misconceptions that have kept you alone,
all these doubts that keep you chained to your home,
they're just a kind of static
that you no longer need.
With clarity now, you decide
to make the fear fear you.

SOMETHING I KNOW FOR SURE

She says the world is simply light and vibration,
wrapped around an idea
that someone had, so many years ago.
In a whisper she informs me
that it's all supposed to be rainbows,
but sometimes rainbows falter
and fall like shooting stars.

Her smile is wide and open,
her eyes shine more than mine,
and she dances in her own world
where rainbows rule the sky.

If there is a god,
I hope she is like that.

ANDREW'S SON

You look at me
through familiar eyes,
and you see these sad eyes
caught deep in memory and sorrow.
You are carefree,
full of energy and curiosity,
eager to learn and keen to try.
I see this all at a glance,
and you are all of three years old.

Buried on a warm day
amidst a shower of tears and mourning,
Andrew left this world.
Leaving behind (for me)
high school memories of friendship, baseball, perseverance,
and the idea that I can be a better man.

AVIAN DANCE – A MEMORY POEM

From above,
the world is shapeless,
with nothing more than a slight curve
at the edges of the horizon
and a blended mix of colour
that continues to bring joy to her eye.
The eagle breathes majestically through the air,
diving and rising upon the thermal currents.
She circles rainbows and storm clouds
and the warmth she feels within
endlessly comforts her.
This high up she is untouchable,
and the echo of her heartbeat
is the drum that guides the world.

She wears a blue dress
and it is down around her waist.
She dances high upon the platform,
a slow seductive movement
that is subtle to the eye.
Her breasts are pale and small,
and her ribs are visible,
looking eerily like the bones in a bird's wings.

THE DISTANT ECHO OF THUNDER

The distant echo of thunder
raises you from exhausted sleep,
for the memories of troubled youth
always return with the rain.

She stands in the street
wearing faded pyjamas
and clinging to a soft toy
that meant something once.
The storm rages around her,
yet she remains calm and quiet,
her youthful face wet and full of sorrow
but even that is intangible.

With tears in his weary eyes
the sadness swells within him,
to the point where he fears
that it will overwhelm
all that he is.
He fears that it has already done
the same for her.

Her voice,
when it finally comes
is lost beneath the distant echo of thunder.

SAM'S SONG

The light in her eyes is so brilliant
that it catches you off guard
the first time you see her.

You see the way he looks at her,
the way he brushes her hair aside,
and you can't deny there is something there.
The light in her eyes,
that easy smile,
it's like she has always been there.
In any situation,
every varied scene,
she is comfortable and carefree.
Shooting stars do not surprise her,
she sees them every day.
In him you see someone
who can give her everything she deserves.

The light in her eyes is brilliant,
truly radiant,
and you find yourself in a prayer,
that it will never fade.

SACRIFICE

They nailed him to the tree
with spikes of sharpened bone,
carved runes upon his face
and left him there to bleed.

At dusk on the third day,
as the sun turned heavy and red,
the tree began to change.
Its wide trunk cracked,
bark parting like tallow flesh,
amber sap dripping sluggish and slow.

Bloodless and dry,
the body slipped from its final embrace
and dropped to the ground like a spent leaf.
From the yawning maw of the ritual tree
there stepped a deity,
summoned to flesh to raise fertility in a dying world.
He stood for a time and surveyed the pale vista
and the empty tourmaline sky.
He shook his head slowly
and with a prolonged release of pent breath
offered no excuse for his resignation.
Behind him, the tree shrank and shrivelled,
consuming the dead husk of the sacrifice

as it retreated into the ground.

Later, when hope had again fled the land,
there came a man with scars upon his face.

SALLY'S PRAYER

Sally says that maybe darkness is just another form of light,
only it's afraid to shine, just like the rest of us.
She admits, that in quiet moments,
she offers up a prayer for those who have gone,
and those that have stayed behind.
She describes it as a thoughtless sorrow,
heart shaped and hollow,
that sits in the soul like a hunger.

Sally says that sometimes,
in the darkness,
the thought that keeps her alive
is a simple one.
For if she can find light in darkness,
surely she can find hope in life.

AN ETERNAL QUEEN

White like an intangible mist,
like a silken shroud,
like a dead eye.
She waits within like a whisper,
like a rumour,
like a promise to be made.

Cold as a grave,
as a lost love,
as a life unlived.
She calls for me as an answer,
as a friend,
as a forgotten foe.

Dark of the dilated pupil,
of an obsidian blade,
of an unbroken vow.
She sings to me of an ending,
of a beginning,
of a soul's worth.

With involuntary enthusiasm,
I step into the white.
Into the cold.
Into the dark.

She appears ghostlike and still,
a loving, horrible, irrevocable smile
upon those flawless ivory features.
And in her hand she holds an arrow,
it's head already red with my heart's blood,
though it had not yet pierced my skin.
With an opaque sigh I become one
with the white, the cold, the dark.

LATE ON A SUNDAY

Watching her approach
makes me think of starless nights,
bushlands after fires,
and my own failings as a man.

A sarong of ochre and brown
blends into her skin,
giving an animalistic image.
In passing, she nods briefly, and barely smiles.
Her obsidian eyes are wide,
they carry mystery instead of self-pity,
and the set of her shoulders remains firm.
When you next look, she is further down the street,
carried away on bone-thin legs
and a gait that makes you think of tribesmen.

Watching her depart
makes me think of the cost of misinterpretation,
the weight of our fears
and the potential for rejuvenation.

ON CALVARY HILL

At dusk, on Calvary Hill,
when everything was done
and the sun began to bleed against the horizon,
a pair of crows turned twigs in the pale grass,
searching for grubs and God knows what else.
They leave the way they came,
unsatisfied and lacking.

Nothing has changed for them.
No great monument of history
etched in either stone or memory.

As they depart across a fading cloudless sky,
the crows caw like children who know truth,
and yet, in true simplicity,
dusk continues to fall on Calvary Hill.

WOUNDS OF THE MIND

He recalls a war,
but his mind has built trenches and barricades
between him and those memories.
He is too old to be plagued by such things,
but its spell lies over him still.
The wounds of the mind do not heal
like those of the flesh,
if they heal at all.

The city streets are cold,
even in summer.
He has grown beyond the need for companionship,
although he would still welcome it,
if he remembered how.
He lives his life on silver coins,
wandering daze-like,
trapped in the days of his youth.
The defences of his mind
have been torn down and overrun.

He does not see society,
wouldn't understand it if he could.
He spends his nights
under the shadow of those old stars
that he brought back with him from half a world away,

trying to decide which voices are real.

For days he has felt it all coming together.
Then, late one night he awakens
and he sees a young girl walking towards him.
He knows her as a shadow of his mind.
As she approaches
he sees something familiar in the Asian cast of her eyes.
She smiles at him,
and through all the years he remembers.
As his tears begin to fall, she reaches out
and with the grace of the young, the broken,
and the light behind the world,
she touches his arm.
He can see forgiveness in her eyes.

With a slow sigh he releases all his pain.
In quiet thanks,
he closes his eyes for a moment.
When he opens them,
everything is illuminated.

LEVIATHAN – A MEMORY POEM

The world is blue below
and blue above.
She moves through the deep places
in vivid, majestic glory.
Her song echoes through the oceans
as she sings the beginnings of all things.
Her soul searches for the others,
binds them together with old magic
that is almost gone from the world.
She sings to them of their beginnings
and of the battle to come.

She spends her time on the beaches,
looking out to sea.
There is something captivating
about the wide blue shimmering surface
that calls to her in a song
with a music she has tried to replicate in her own.
So she spends her time on the beaches,
another failed musician
searching for the answers.

REVENANTS OF YOUTH

A slow sunset,
the last echo of another solemn day.
Somehow the trees seem greener.
The grass in the park across the road calls to you,
whispers to you of your childhood.
Reminds you of hours spent watching clouds
cascading across a crystalline sky
that seemed so damn big.
Memories of dirty hands and scraped knees,
footy games on the front lawn
and fights over girlfriends or plastic army men
that seemed so bloody important.
So Adam's moved away now
and we don't see each other anymore.

And how the years work their magic,
taking the little things that we used to cherish
and replacing them with responsibilities, jobs, and debt.
The slow curse of time,
if you want to look at it that way.

Unexpectedly,
I saw Adam at the baseball park.
Both of us older now,
at this place where we used to play,

where now our children play.
We're both bearded and married,
wiser and probably a little dumber in some ways.
More patient and less enthusiastic perhaps
than we were as kids.
For a moment the years stand between us like stone,
and then the realisation hits,
swells for a moment and becomes something more real.
All those times,
those shared experiences that cannot be replaced,
resurface.
They flood the mind with warm emotion.
A nostalgia that does not abate,
but creates in its place something new,
something that will remain,
undaunted,
a remnant of innocence retained,
a revenant of youth.

IMMORTAL – A MEMORY POEM

He traces city streets,
stalks alleyways and back roads.
There is darkness everywhere
and he feels hopelessness consuming him.
Yet he pushes himself on,
the need for redemption burning inside
like an endless flame.
It shows through in those swirling yellow eyes
as the panther moves from shadow to shadow.

It is dark in Forrand Park
and the streetlights seem so far away.
He sits on a park bench,
scratches the inside of a finger with his thumbnail
and dwells in his regrets.
He closes his eyes,
tries to wrap oblivion around himself like a dark cloak.
Pain burns within his mind,
over-filled as it is with memories, self-doubt and missed
                                             opportunities.
These failures he cannot escape,
echo in his mind in torment
of the destiny he needs to find.
He opens his eyes
takes a breath of the cool winter air

and tries once more to start anew.

The night is dark, and he is invisible within it,
stalking through the tree-lined mountain slopes.
The full moon is distant and small,
yet in its pale light his god appears
with gifts, curses, and secrets
that were never meant to be spoken.
Something shifts within
and the panther becomes something more.
He stands upon two feet,
peers into the face of the one who has remade him,
and as he begins to understand,
his screams echo through the night.

THE LAST DAY OF HISTORY

A boy,
teenage and full of possibility,
wakes early on a Sunday morning.
With surfboard in hand
he makes his way beneath a passive purple sky.

Pale sand, nestled against the slumbering city,
where the world seems a peaceful place.
The boy pushes the cold surface sand aside
to sit and watch the surf.
He enjoys the solitude and peace
that surrounds him at times like this.

The sun rises,
slow and orange,
above the western horizon.
The cold side of Perth's buildings
feels the warmth of the dawn sun
for the first time in history
on the last day of history.

BLACKENED LEAVES

Early morning, still dark,
and the fox stares back at you,
marble eyes opaque and judgeless.
The headlights wash past,
and the fox flees,
another shadow in suburbia.

Afternoon, and there is ash in the air,
the sun is a glowing red ember in a smoke-stained sky
and blackened leaves float down eerily,
like feathers from a black winged bird.
You stand on the patio,
look out over the houses to the bushland,
so close and so fragile.
So dry.

A breeze, edged with cold,
has cleared the smoke for now.
The grass crunches beneath your feet
and on the back lawn,
clear evidence of a visitor the night before,
is a headless pile of skin, fur and bone.

Like woodland after a bushfire
all that was, will be again.

LEAVING HOSPITAL HOPES

IV DUSK

Walled by hurricane fencing
and construction vehicles,
the new hospital slowly rises,
ringed in scaffolding and expectant helplessness.
An unwanted journey
or a hopeful destination.

The beautiful and painful symmetry
of a baby's first cry
and a grandmother's last breath.

Beneath the reach of a towering crane
and a semi-translucent moon,
the building wraps itself in dusk
like a grieving wife in memory.

And somewhere near, a crow caws,
a singular echo of sadness.

V DARKNESS

In the night the hospital looms monumental,
dwarfing the ancient structure
that it has been built up around.
This modern castle of hope,
a tower of desperation.
The palace of pain and perseverance.

There is a song within the silence,
an echo of everything that was.
It whispers on a night wind,
a lingering memory of hope.
For all that is not fought for
is everything that falls away.

VI DAWN

As morning spreads its weary fingers across her face
those inside wake,
relieved, relaxed or revered.
The light of angels is little seen these days,
but to one who knows to look,
the air above the hospital
is a dazzling rainbow of majestic light.
A shimmering haze that marks the passage
between life and death.
Buried beneath the sight of such wonder,
pain flutters and falls away.
Grief becomes a sweet emotion
and sorrow sings a song that is eventually uplifting.
The sun rises, again.

DREAM GATES

At night,
within her slumber,
she softly traces the pathways
that lead through gates of stone
gates of wood
and gates of wonder.

In waking hours,
the remembered colours of dreaming
show through in her open smile.
The vibrations of her nightly journeys
reflect the stories her father used to tell
and through her,
brings joy to those she meets.

KYPROULLA'S GARDEN

-for Angelo

At the top of a hill in Bradbury
you see roses before a simple redbrick house.
On the patio there are always lounges or plastic chairs
and an ashtray on a coffee table covered by a white cloth.
For fear of being wrong I do not name the ferns and flowers
and the trees that grace the gardens or line the driveway,
yet their greenery and the love put into them so precisely
and with so much warmth,
passes into me, every time I'm there.

But years later,
when we're older and tired and not as enthusiastic,
I drive past that old house.
The flowers are all gone.
The patio is free from lounges.
There is no sound of laughter, or tears,
or words spoken in another language
that you can almost understand.
It recalls to me the memories
of a house so filled with love,
and the remnants of a mother,
her pride, her loyalty, her warmth of heart.
There is so much in the fragrance of Kyproulla's roses,

that all these years later,
when I drive past that house on Akuna,
I can still see them in my mind.

CITY SILENT

Sally wakes in a dream,
finds the city silent
and wanders down wide unpopulated streets
where there are no streetlights or sirens.
No bass.
No neon.
Even the hum of electricity is absent.

She finds herself wishing
that she could find this sort of solitude
in her everyday life,
without the nagging presence of loneliness
that only leaves her when she sleeps.

Sally makes her way north,
between the taller buildings,
finds herself looking at The Harbour Bridge,
a dark silhouette against an enormous starlit sky.
She turns in a circle,
staring at the beauty of the moonlight
reflecting over steel and glass
as it slowly revolves around her.
She hides the sorrow she feels
at the thought of waking up.

SUNSET SILHOUETTES

Beneath the dusk sun and the long, yellowed sky,
he studies the stretching silhouettes
and thinks of the place where he grew up.
Edged by bushland, with that scent of dust on the wind
when the rain grew near.
The stillness of a summer afternoon,
when even the flies were too buggered to bother anyone.
It makes him think of his family,
spread out and not so close anymore,
and he slowly wipes a tear from his cheek.

As you grow older,
so too do the days,
and they stretch like those same silhouettes at dusk.

AN OCTOBER DIRGE

-for Cameron

You can hear the roll of bagpipes
and a subtle violin,
it echoes through the halls of your mind
as memories resurface, swirl and ebb away.
The waiting is painfully timeless,
becomes a vigil,
and the music in your mind becomes a dirge.
The hospital ward is quiet,
but for the whirl and beep of cold machines,
and the slow rasp of a final breath.
Your mother saw you into this world,
so it's only fitting that you see her out.

Years from now,
Octobers find you restless,
they leave you looking at that loss,
a cathartic twist of regret and love,
and you may never feel whole again,
but like a stone cast across a smooth river surface,
the ripples of her life flow into yours,
and through each chaotic day,
and every quiet moment,
she is always with you.

MEMORY - A MEMORY POEM

He took her to Africa
because she always loved the big cats.
They watch as a leopard
bounds into the reaching grasp of an acacia tree,
and they stare in awe as giraffe move fluidly
across the path of the jeep.
The tour guide slows the vehicle
and points out elephants in the distance.
Deep within her soul
she feels something shift,
and it makes her shiver with something akin to recognition.
It tickles at the corner of her mind,
and with a sense of foreboding,
she begins to remember.

She stands at the edge of the herd,
ears and tail flick in one distinct motion.
Beneath the guard of the older elephants
the young ones splash and roll in the water.
She watches, surveys the savannah,
recalling the beginning, and therefore the last end.
She sees the darkness growing in the north,
high on the mountain slope where the ice forms.
She looks to the young once more
and in empathy, mourns their innocence.

SECRETS

Amy is cute.
She has dark orange hair
that is done in dreadlocks.
She wears trendy, skater-kid clothes.
Amy has big boobs.
She hasn't told her boyfriend that she also likes girls,
or that one day, she wants to be a lawyer.
She's comfortable,
and more than anything,
Amy likes that feeling.
In quiet times,
she wonders if it's so wrong to protect that.

THE DARK BETWEEN THE STARS

Late autumn,
caught between the seasons,
the air has a tendency to change
just before sunset,
when the world begins to cold.

He is sitting on the balcony,
wearing shorts and worn slippers,
drinking beer by himself.
He shivers beneath the oncoming twilight,
looks to the setting sun,
and thinks of her.
It is an invisible weight
that crushes down upon him.
In his mind he is a stooped man,
shoulders bent beneath the doubts and heartache
that plague his daily life.
He is younger than he feels,
better looking than he believes,
yet he distances himself from others,
becoming the hermit he is convinced he should be.

At night,
melancholy and warm from alcohol,

he finds it hard to breathe.
He stares at the city lights,
these silent human constellations
in a disassociated night.
With a sigh he lets his gaze drift
up to the pristine obsidian sky.
For a moment that constant burden lifts,
the bands around his chest loosen and temporarily depart.
He takes a deep breath of frigid winter air,
and as the cold hits his lungs he thinks of Heaven.
He wonders if she is up there somewhere,
watching, from the dark between the stars.

PEDESTAL

A crow sits like a forgotten idol
on a garbage bin out for collection.
His own personal stinking pedestal,
picking at the pieces that jut out beneath the lid.

Bow, if you dare
to the totem of all and nothing,
stranded in a world
that cannot recall its own origins.

At dusk,
crow-call echoes across the city skyline
yet there are none who hear it
for all that it really is.

Bow, if you dare.

SILENT ANGEL

Sensing movement,
I look in the rear-view,
but there is nothing there,
just some other cars
and their overly bright headlights.

Driving home,
I'm tired and a little depressed,
making characters in my mind
to stay awake.

Instinctively,
I glance at the rear-view once more
and she is there,
looking back at me with vivid eyes
that see within me.
Golden hair frames her beautiful face
and the trailing headlights
create a perfect halo.

She sees within me,
and neither smiles nor frowns.
She simply looks at me
until I look away.

Later, alone at the computer,
I am inspired to write.

AN UNDERSTATED ANTHEM

A desolate street,
a torn umbrella
spinning and flapping
in a brisk breeze like a broken crow.
She walks with her head held high,
this little girl with too much life experience,
and too much hurt inside,
but too much pride to hide it.
People watch from their windows
scared and unable to speak.
She keeps going,
an echo of her lingers behind
in each unabated step.
Those who watch wonder
and wish for something more.
The girl keeps looking for it.

GREEN CROW

In the summer he is invisible among the leaves,
and he watches over everything.
Autumn arrives and his feathers mottle
to burning red and gold.
His gaze pierces humanity, studying and learning.
Winter creeps in on old legs.
He loses weight and his feathers fall out,
his wings looking eerily like dead branches,
yet still he watches,
enjoying the drama of life.
Spring returns and you hear his caw
rising above the seasons.
You look up,
but he is invisible among the greenery.

THOSE WHO WERE LEFT BEHIND

-for the Finns & the Rumsbys

Amongst the heartache and the doubts,
the daily reminders and the sadnesses,
people often forget the weight that lays upon
those who were left behind.
There's nothing you can say
no words can heal that pain,
but a hug, the warmth of sunlight,
an afternoon breeze on a summer day,
tears shared in a lounge room,
those things go a long way,
and someday,
whilst the memories remain
the pain is not so sharp.
It's a sadness but a truth
that the sun rises every day,
and only those who were left behind
are here to see it.

EVERY BREATH IS A CIRCLE

Upon the cold horizon,
a frozen sun forlorn,
neither rising nor able to fall.
An eternal golden moment,
bringing mothers to tears,
newborns to silence,
and grandparents to know the truth,
that after all the long enduring years,
every single ending
is another beginning begun.

SALLY

Sally breaks down
and still she tries not to cry.
All the hope and faith
that she has been collecting
begins to whisper away,
like crumpled leaves on a cold wind.

There is nothing more hopeless
than watching something break
that you cannot fix,
when with all your heart
all you want is to put it back together again.
So I try to wait,
wanting to comfort her through it all,
but how can I do that,
when I'm as messed up as she is.

Sally takes a handful of pills,
waits for the world to go numb,
and wonders if she wants to wake up at all.

CROW – A MEMORY POEM

He's been travelling for years,
pulling con-jobs and scams wherever he goes.
He takes what he needs – food, shelter, women, booze –
with an ease that marvels even himself.
Sleight of hand and an innate ability to read people
sees him through almost every situation.
Yet there is a hole inside him,
a pit of darkness that he fears can never be filled.
He looks up at the wide blue sky and wonders
if there is something that he has been missing.

Blue on black, like midnight,
an ink-stain in a field of vibrant heather.
Taking his fill of carrion, he pauses,
cocks his head to the side and wonders
if what he hears is an end
or just another beginning.
Suddenly aware of the descending shadow,
he shuffles a few awkward steps and takes flight,
cawing wildly as he climbs into the bright blue sky.

CHILDHOOD VIGNETTE

And so I walk,
nostalgic,
around the neighbourhood where I grew up,
as a warm wind in from Wedderburn
carries the smell of smoke to my nose.

Sifting through the years of my childhood.
I rub leaves between my fingers
and drift back with the moist richness of the earth.
I walk back towards my childhood,
with tears
slowly tracing their way down my face.
I walk through these old dark trees
that we used to play in after school,
the thin bark crunches beneath my feet
and I am bombarded by carefree memories.

Later, I find myself down at the baseball park,
and I jump the fence and wander around.
The pitcher's mound seems smaller,
and the dirt at second base
smells just as good as it always did.
I head out to the outfield,
and I slowly look up.
There is nothing quite like a baseball

as it descends from a clear blue saturday sky.

I sit upon the ground
up in the reserve near where I live
and I watch as the sun casts long shadows.
There is a tree where we used to play cricket,
but right now four young kids
practise at golf
with clubs that are way too big.
I feel like I should tell them
to hold onto each other,
because friendship
is the richest thing in the world.

There is magic in these memories
that I will not forget.
There is history and love and warmth
that will stay with me,
and hopefully, many years from now,
I will still remember.

THE PHOENIX REDEMPTION

Phoenix fell for an eternity,
the days and nights flashing past
in a cascading array of darknesses and lights
that left him dizzy and reeling.
Eventually, on a starless night,
he came to a stop in a field somewhere,
the lights of a city in the distance.
He heard the cicadas and the night birds in the trees,
found himself excited and nervous at the same time.
This world was new to him, enormous and full of wonder.
He couldn't wait to see it all.

IN TRIUMPH

He has magic in his veins
and all the power of a superhero resides within him.
He wanders through parking lots,
talking to cars and waiting for them to reply...
He scratches at the concrete,
trying to get to the mica
because it is pretty to his eye.

He has magic in his veins,
and often, he thinks about sharing it.
But he cannot see humanity
through the greed, anger, violence, rage
and intolerance that surrounds him.

One night,
in contemplating the state of it all,
he looks up at the stars and recalls,
how when he was younger,
they were so much brighter.
In triumph he smiles and gives everything
to the dark night sky.

ENDINGS AND BEGINNINGS – A MEMORY POEM

Upon the mountain peak,
in the shadow of the ice wall,
she comes upon the dark reflection of herself.
She looks upon the lioness,
so like herself, yet black as ebony
with knowing soulless eyes.
A malignant evil, clawing back into the world
with only darkness in its pounding heart.
The lioness feels the presence of the other totems within her.
This threat of darkness has not gone unnoticed,
and with their power behind her,
she attacks.

Sam wakes from a vivid dream
that she recognises as a memory from another life.
She sits in the dark, sweating profusely.
The lingering sense of that long ago evil,
banished and held down for so long,
is slowly rising again.
Limbs like probing tentacles,
slowly regathering its strength.
And now that she knows of it,
she cannot look away.
She rises, packs a bag quickly and leaves the apartment.

The morning is cold and there is frost on her windshield,
as she starts the car she can only hope
that once again the others will follow...

DON'T LIVE YOUR LIFE LIKE A DIRGE

Mother,
can you see me,
putting all the pieces of myself back together
as best I can,
seeing if there's enough there
to hold some holy light.
In a daze, I remember myself
in your arms,
as pure as I ever was or will be.
Such a serene memory
bubbling back into my existence.

Brother,
Remind me of the song
we sang as children,
by the pool and in the sun,
in the yard or at the park
Running and squealing and full of joy.
Can you still see the sunlight
glistening across rippling water?
Or that glorious shaft of light at sunset?
Heaven isn't where we go when we die,
we're born into it.

Sister,
What is the tune of your soul
and where did you hear it loudest?
If strength is an art then you are an artist.
I named my first born for you.
You let me grow in a world of dragons,
and raised me into the cerulean sky.
Your breath lingers eternally in my ear.

Father,
can you feel me,
following and leading,
such an intricate act of life,
in this collective kaleidoscope of souls.
All that you know is known,
and all that you regret is long forgiven.
Alas, as the light gets ever brighter,
give me the strength to look,
and the bravery to look away.

RUNWAYS

After school, kids play baseball
at the park down the road.
Cleo and I walk past them
every Friday afternoon.
Slowly, the sun begins to set,
sending spears of orange, pink and purple light
slashing across the thin clouds
and that endless blue sky.
The kids pick up their gear
and drift away
to T.V, and dinner,
and homework.

Sometimes,
when that field has gone dark,
I take the pup with me
and we head down there.

At nighttime,
the streetlights here just seem to stretch on forever,
reminding me of runways.

There is a big old gum
- with dry green leaves,
thick branches and a pale trunk -

that we sit beneath.
I give the girl her lead
and she dances joyously around me,
nipping at my fingers
and licking my face,
- she is still learning to bark,
and the soft noises that she comes out with make me smile.
I play with her for a bit with an old tennis ball
before I lay down
to stare up at that tree-broken, star-smashed Macarthur sky,
and remember dreams I had when I was young.

URBAN MYTHOLOGY

Let me tell you a story
of a house that is a forest within.
Of a cat that takes away your pain,
whenever you're in need.
Or a possum who was once a girl,
or a girl, who was once a crow.
There's a house on Temple St
that is a haven for homeless kids,
or a red brick apartment building atop a hill
with lounges in the backyard,
where stories are told like something sacred.
There's a painting in the gallery,
that is a doorway to another world,
where memory waits to be remembered.
There's a forgotten god in a cafe
and a strange little shop
that stocks a little bit of everything,
where a stone dragon sneaks
and plays between aisles of second hand books.
There are musicians who invoke magic with their music
and so very much more.
Welcome to Westreach

THE BLACK CATHEDRAL

In a restless dream you walk,
up steps of polished obsidian,
between columns of dark marble
streaked with veins like silver and golden lightning.
Heavy ebony doors open before you,
and upon entering,
you gaze upon stained glass windows
depicting shadowed animals
amidst the violent forces of nature.
A wolf in a snowstorm.
A lioness beneath momentous thunderheads.
A bear braced before the tempest of a wildfire.
A crow fleeing a hurricane,
and so many more.

Within, the floor is an inky pupil,
opaque and smooth,
like the surface of a primal lake,
All-Knowing and inconceivably vast.
Upon it, a range of varied figures stand,
wearing the heads of totems that remain
as remnants in their blood.

Behold the Black Cathedral,
the structure of all eternity,

buried beneath your heartbeat,
-The Temple of Forever.

WINDRUSH

by Rick Neilsen

The wind shall be your friend
and blow goodwill to you.
May your eyes be filled with laughter,
maybe a tear or two.
Remember the good things we did,
the places we have been.
The sun and moon,
the stars and all the shades of green,
clouds of fluffy white, stormy black rain,
icy cold nights all alone,
remembering my warm love for the future,
the past, the here and now.
Will you remember me?

CREDITS

COVER DESIGNER

    Elizabeth McCracken of Coven Press
    Cover imagery by Adobe Stock
    Titles: Azo Sans
    Blurb: Adobe Jenson Pro

INTERNAL FORMATTING

    Alana Lambert of Coven Press
    Body: Adobe Text Pro/12pt/16pt Leading
    Heading: Waters Titling Pro/18pt/16pt Leading

www.ingramcontent.com/pod-product-compliance
Lightning Source LLC
Chambersburg PA
CBHW072014290426
44109CB00018B/2233